THE WHEEL OF THE YEAR SERIES

PREMONITION
— DESIGNS —

Fleurdelys
COVENSTEAD

EST. 2017

pine
&
parchment

CHILDREN'S INTRO TO
LITHA

AN ILLUSTRATED GUIDE

BY LIAM CAREW

The sun is high and bright,
the trees are lush and green.
The air is warm, the sky is blue,
a beautiful summer scene.

The forest is alive with animal chatter,
rushing waters wash away worries.
A season of power, rest, and independence...
Litha is here in all of its glory!

Let's begin celebrating by honoring some animals!
After all, the creatures of Litha are magical!

Up first, Ladybugs, the resilient protectors,
guardians of plants and flowers.
They use scent to ward away other pests,
demonstrating the importance
of embracing your individual power.

Bright in color with black speckled spots,
bold and unashamed of who they are!
A lesson on being unapologetically you,
because to someone else,
you may be their idol or star!

Ladybugs are seen as messengers of luck,
you feel fortunate when one comes your way.
How can you be more like a Ladybug?
Start by being a blessing in someone else's day!

Horses are creatures of strength and beauty,
they are powerhouses much like the sun.
They teach us that through hard work,
there's no job we cannot get done!

Horses symbolize freedom,
there is no obstacle they cannot defeat;
They don't run away to escape their problems,
but instead, march towards the solution
with each hoofbeat.

There is a spirit of confidence and pride,
something we can all admire and appreciate.
A reminder that it's okay
to showcase your strengths,
as long as it's balanced by humility and grace.

Frogs are creatures of transformation,
born in water as helpless tadpoles.
They go through a major metamorphosis,
to sprout legs, grow, and become whole!
Just because you are who you are today,
doesn't mean your story is done being told!

A Frog has mastery over both land and pond,
they can hop to impressive heights
and swim at top speeds.
A lesson that you might be
more resourceful than you think,
if you just embrace who you were meant to be!

Litha is a reminder to relax,
and what better way than to listen to song...
The Frogs will croak and ribbit harmoniously,
singing their healing tune all day long.

Hummingbirds are a flighty little sight,
their energy is vibrant and free.
They are playful and joyful, colorful and light,
always treating themselves to something sweet!
Although we can't always be like Hummingbirds,
there are totally moments where we should be!

Don't let their stature defy you,
their wanderlust and courage are quite large!
Showing us to be fearless adventurers,
and in unwary circumstances,
do not be afraid to take charge!

Hummingbirds are seen as symbols of resilience,
they overcome so much to simply exist.
Even with limited food options,
a rapid heartbeat, and a super tiny size...
They're still kind and gentle despite it.

The vibrancy of nature is in full bloom...
How we dress should certainly match!
It's best to be in sync with the colors around us,
let's use tie dye to do just that!

Although you can absolutely rely on tie dye kits,
or even resort to the food coloring trick...
There are natural ways to create dyes,
and I'll teach you just how to do it!

For blue, collect blueberries and elderberries.
Pink, you'll need strawberries or beets.
Yellow comes from carrots or turmeric.
Oh, and avocado skins and pits make peach!
Purple from red cabbage, basil, or huckleberry.
And lastly, use grass or spinach to make green!

Grind ingredients and soak in water overnight.
Then, boil and reduce until half the liquid is gone.
Strain out any solids, add in some alum,
pour into squeeze bottles for some tie dye fun!

Another way to embrace color,
and use nature as your base,
is by painting stones and rocks,
adding character to your outdoor space.

Some like to paint their favorite animals,
or perhaps a beautiful landscape.
Others just paint them to be solid colors,
in simple patterns, or decorate with shapes!

Then there's my personal favorite...
Painting them in bright neon shades,
writing an inspiring message or quote on top...
A great way to brighten up someone else's day!

Okay, what are you going for?
A color, a message, a shape, or
an animal you adore?

Okay, one more colorful exercise...
It's a gratifying, challenging activity, too!
You must create and complete
a rainbow matching board;
I just know this is something you can do!

You must match flowers, plants,
and other forms of nature,
to the multiple colors on the board.
Try your hardest to get them all,
and have a prize for the person
with the top score!

Look around at the scene we have here.
My board has eight colors that I must match,
I already see a blue feather and pink flowers...
Can you pair up items and colors just as fast?!

Relaxation is a major element of Litha,
but conversely, so is movement and power...
So what better way to honor
those otherwise contradicting themes,
than to swim or splash for a couple hours!?

Now you don't need a pool to do this,
you can use the beach, a pond, or a lake.
With adult supervision you can float and relax,
or play exciting, yet safe, swimming games!

If you don't have a way to swim
or haven't yet learned,
embrace your sprinkler or hose!
Add in some bubbles, make a splash pad,
or even just dance in a sun shower, I suppose!

Although it isn't yet time for dessert,
it's vital we stay cool in the summer sun.
Let's make some fruit infused popsicles!
Hydration and creativity, all in one!

But what does this have to do with Litha?
Well...don't see them as treats,
see them as frozen little potions!
We use ingredients for both
their flavors and their properties,
to infuse these popsicles with some intention
and metaphysical devotion!

Apples for love, watermelon for joy,
kiwi for health, blueberries for honesty.
Mango for confidence, orange for growth,
pomegranate for luck, and lemon for clarity.

Which combination will you choose?
Which of those flavors or properties
are most important to you?

Litha is when the sun's energy is at its height,
it's the perfect time to create pendants...
We harness the strength of the solstice,
and make jewelry to bless and enchant.

You can choose any stone or crystal,
carve a sigil into wood
or make something out of clay.
Just be sure to consider intention and symbolism,
so that the energy you are seeking
can easily come your way.

After you assemble your amulet,
take it outside and find a place for it to rest.
In the sunlight it will charge,
and when you wear it, what you wished for,
will surely manifest!

Warm breezes now fill our days,
carrying the sounds of nature along.
By making and hanging up a wind chime,
we can contribute to summer's song!

You can use almost anything solid
to make a wind chime;
Upcycling old silverware, buttons,
or even sea shells.
Affix them to string
and dangle from an upper ring,
then place them anywhere the wind swells.

Wind chimes are said to cleanse a space,
known to purify an area
and send good vibes all around.
They are also thought to enhance energy,
just like the sun does,
except instead, with sound!

We've done so much,
I'm sure you've worked up quite the appetite.
On Litha we eats lots of grilled foods,
paired with beverages that are light and bright!

First up, hot dogs and burgers,
paired with all the condiments and fix ins.
Plus a plethora of zesty pasta salads,
and grilled vegetables nicely seasoned.

A couple of steaks with beautiful char lines;
An assortment of skewers made with
veggies, shrimp, chicken, or beef
Freshly made herbed potato medley,
and salad to provide us with essential greens.

Don't worry, the grill will remain on,
So if you're still hungry...
There's more where that came from!

Where has the time gone!?
The day has begun to fade.
All these sunny activities have made me tired,
it's best we find a comfy spot in the shade.

Relaxing outdoors is good for the soul,
it is proven to increase one's happiness,
Especially while swaying in a hammock...
This will eliminate most anxiety and stress.

While you lay there and drift off,
remember that Litha is a time to just be.
How can you better embrace independence?
In what ways do you need to
let go of worries and set yourself free?

After a nice, enlightening nap,
I hope you're ready for a delicious snack!
I sure am, so let's see what we've got...

There are treats that will cool you off,
like these assorted ice cream sundaes!
Or fresh baked desserts to warm you up,
like this berry pie with its sugary glaze.

Freshly chopped watermelon ready to enjoy,
orange and grapefruit danishes galore.
Raspberry cookies by the dozen,
and a ton of marshmallows and s'mores!

A fig or two for something subtly sweet,
pistachio-almond torrone, such a sticky delight.
Hazelnut cremes and buttery shortbread,
with marble cookies baked just right!
Is it time to dig in?!
Cause this is the perfect way to end the night!

Happy Litha,
to you and yours!

Blessed Be
and Good Night.

Made in United States
North Haven, CT
27 March 2024

50588259R00020